TOP 10:
VENOM

By Virginia Loh-Hagan

45th Parallel Press

Published in the United States of America by Cherry Lake Publishing
Ann Arbor, Michigan
www.cherrylakepublishing.com

Content Adviser: Stephen Ditchkoff, Professor of Wildlife Ecology and Management, Auburn University, Alabama
Reading Adviser: Marla Conn, ReadAbility, Inc.
Book Designer: Melinda Millward

Photo Credits: ©Subaqueosshutterbug/iStockphoto, cover, 1, 21; ©Mauro Rodrigues/Shutterstock Images, 5; ©Adam Ke/ Shutterstock Images, 6; ©Yann hubert/Shutterstock Images, 7; © Klaus / http://www.flickr.com/ CC BY-SA 2.0, 8; © Dave Watts / Alamy Stock Photo, 9; ©worldswildlifewonders/Shutterstock Images, 10; ©Kris Wiktor/Shutterstock Images, 12; ©Design Pics/ Thinkstock, 12; ©Kunal Mehta/Shutterstock Images, 12; ©reptiles4all/Shutterstock Images, 13; ©Aleks Kend/Shutterstock Images, 14; ©LIU JIXING/Shutterstock Images, 14; ©Cuson/Shutterstock Images, 14; ©AlekseyKarpenko/Shutterstock Images, 15; ©EcoPrint/Shutterstock Images, 16; ©POPUMON/Shutterstock Images, 16; ©Milan Vachal/Shutterstock Images, 16; © Nico Smit/Dreamstime.com, 17; ©Roman Vintonyak/Shutterstock Images, 18; ©Ethan Daniels/Shutterstock Images, 18; ©Andrea Izzotti/Shutterstock Images, 18; © Jxpfeer /Dreamstime.com, 19; ©Teguh Tirtaputra/Shutterstock Images, 20; © Oksanavg / Dreamstime.com, 20; ©Jette Vis/Shutterstock Images, 22; ©Suede Chen/Shutterstock Images, 23; © Astrid Gast/Dreamstime. com, 24; ©Cyhel/Shutterstock Images, 24, 25; ©LauraD/Shutterstock Images, 24; ©Rich Carey/Shutterstock Images, 26; ©Divelvanov/iStockphoto, 27; ©R. Gino Santa Maria/Shutterstock Images, 28; © Vilainecrevette/Dreamstime.com, 28; ©THEGIFT777/iStockphoto, 29; © Thomas P. Peschak/National Geographic Creative/Corbis, 30

Graphic Element Credits: © tukkki/Shutterstock Images, back cover, front cover, multiple interior pages; © paprika/Shutterstock Images, back cover, front cover, multiple interior pages; © Silhouette Lover/Shutterstock Images, multiple interior pages

45th Parallel Press is an imprint of Cherry Lake Publishing.

Library of Congress Cataloging-in-Publication Data

Loh-Hagan, Virginia, author.
    Top 10: venom / by Virginia Loh-Hagan.
pages cm. — (Wild wicked wonderful)
Summary: "Dive into the Wild Wicked Wonderful world of the animal kingdom with the Top 10: Venom. Written with a high interest level to appeal to a more mature audience and a lower level of complexity with clear visuals to help struggling readers along. Considerate text includes tons of fascinating information and wild facts that will hold the readers' interest, allowing for successful mastery and comprehension. A table of contents, glossary with simplified pronunciations, and index all enhance comprehension."– Provided by publisher.
ISBN 978-1-63470-507-3 (hardcover) — ISBN 978-1-63470-627-8 (pbk.) —
ISBN 978-1-63470-567-7 (pdf) — ISBN 978-1-63470-687-2 (ebook)
1. Poisonous animals–Juvenile literature. 2. Dangerous animals–Juvenile literature. 3. Venom–Juvenile literature. I. Title. II. Title: Venom.

QL100.L65 2016
591.6'5–dc23   2015026859

Printed in the United States of America
Corporate Graphics

About the Author

Dr. Virginia Loh-Hagan is an author, university professor, former classroom teacher, and curriculum designer. She does not like venom. She lives in San Diego with her very tall husband and very naughty dogs. To learn more about her, visit www.virginialoh.com.

TABLE OF CONTENTS

INTRODUCTION

Animals bite. They sting. They use **venom**. Venom is poison that's injected. It's injected under the skin. It harms **victims**. Victims are targets of attacks. Poison causes pain. It makes victims not able to move. It can cause death.

Animals inject poison. They do it for different reasons. They want to **survive**. They want to stay alive. They protect themselves. They fight **predators**. Predators are hunters. But venomous animals need to eat. They inject poison into **prey**. Prey are animals hunted for food.

Some animals have extreme poison. Their poison is bigger. Their poison is better. They have the most exciting venom in the animal world!

There are different types of venom.

chapter one

STINGRAYS

Stingrays live in warm waters. They live all over the world. They have stingers under their tails. They can be more dangerous than sharks. They hurt 50 times more humans.

They bury themselves. They hide in sand. They're hard to see. Victims step on them. Stingrays whip their tails around. Their stingers strike. They dig in deep. They inject poison.

Stingrays have **glands**. Glands are organs that ooze stuff. Their glands have poison. They're at the base of the stingers. Their stingers can be 14 inches (35.5 centimeters) long. They're covered with skin.

Tails help stingrays swim. But their stingers are for protection.

Their stings destroy flesh. Pain comes quickly. Stingray poison can be deadly.

Chapter two

PLATYPUSES

Platypuses live in rivers. They live in Australia. They have duck **bills**. Bills are like beaks. They have mole bodies. They have beaver tails. They have swan feet.

They're built to hunt. They hunt underwater. They swim. Their webbed feet paddle. Their tails steer. They close their eyes. They close their ears. They close their noses. Their bills have special feelers. They feel prey's movements.

Mammals have hair or fur. Most give birth to live young. They feed milk to their young. They're warm-blooded.

Platypus stings feel like 100 hornet stings.

But platypuses are special mammals. They lay eggs. They make poison. Not many mammals do this.

Platypus venom is similar to reptile venom.

Platypus poison can kill dogs. It can't kill humans. But it causes great pain. Skin gets swollen. Victims feel pain for three months.

Only males have poison. They have sharp stingers. They're called **spurs**. Spurs are on their back feet. They're on their heels. They inject poison. The poison is made by glands on their thighs.

Males make poison. They don't make it all year. Only when they're ready to mate. They sting other males. They protect their space. They fight for females. While not mating, they can still use their spurs. They use them to cut. But spurs don't have poison during this time.

HUMANS DO WHAT?!?

In Haiti, it's believed people can become zombies. Zombies are dead people who come back to life. Some people believe it is voodoo magic. Puffer fish are poisonous. Voodoo witches grind up puffer fish. This causes paralysis. Victims can't move. The witches also grind up poisonous toads. This makes victims sleepy. They made a magic powder. This powder makes people look dead. Clairvius Narcisse believed he was a zombie slave. He ate the magic powder. He had fevers. He couldn't breathe. He wasn't able to move. People thought he was dead. He watched his own funeral. Then he was taken from the grave. He was drugged. This drug caused memory loss. He was forced to work on a farm. He worked for several years. One day, the owner died. Narcisse returned to his family. Researchers investigated. They found another explanation. Narcisse's brother drugged him. He did this on purpose. They were fighting over land. His brother wanted to get rid of him.

chapter three
GiLA MONSTERS

Gila monsters are lizards. They make poison. Not many lizards do this. They're special. They're the largest U.S. lizards. They're 2 feet (61 cm) long. They weigh 5 pounds (2.3 kilograms). They're slow. But they strike quickly.

They bite. They hold. They have tight grips. Their teeth are sharp. Their teeth slice open skin. Their teeth can fall off. They can be replaced. They have special spit glands. Their glands make poison. Poison dribbles down their teeth. It drips into open cuts. Gila monsters chew. They drip more spit. This adds more poison. They flip over while biting. This also adds more poison.

Gila monsters don't have enough jaw muscles to inject venom. Poison is in their spit.

Their poison makes victims sick. Victims feel pain. Their organs get damaged. They get cold sweats. They can't move.

chapter four

BEES

Bees have poison. They have a tiny bit. But that's all they need. Bees can be deadly. Some animals are **allergic**. Bee stings bother them. They react badly. An allergy is a highly sensitive response.

Female bees have stingers. Stingers are attached to stomachs. They have a poison **sac**. A sac is like a bag. They have a **lancet**. A lancet is like a needle. It delivers the poison.

Bees sting. They pump poison into skin. Bee poison attacks nerves. It causes pain. It bothers skin. It can harm body parts. It hurts organs. It can cause death.

One in a thousand humans are allergic to bee stings. A human can take 10 bee stings per pound. Five hundred stings could kill a child.

Honeybees' stingers get stuck. They get stuck in bodies. The honeybees' stomachs get pulled off with their stingers. So they die when they sting.

chapter five
SCORPIONS

Scorpions are related to spiders. They have **pincers**. Pincers are claws. They're for grabbing. They're for holding. They have tails. Their tails curve over their backs. Their tails have stingers. Stingers have poison.

All scorpions have poison. Not all scorpions are dangerous. Only about 25 types have powerful poison.

Scorpions control their stings. They control their poison. They can stun. They can kill. Sometimes, they use a little poison. This causes pain. But it doesn't kill. They don't want to waste poison.

Scorpions smell to find food and to hide from danger.

They need to eat. They sting prey. Their poison acts fast. Prey's insides turn into soup. Scorpions suck the soup out.

Chapter six
STONEFiSH

Stonefish live in the Pacific Ocean. They're dangerous. They're very poisonous.

They have 12 to 14 spines. Thick skin covers their spines. Each spine has a poison gland. Their poison causes pain. It stops hearts. It causes death.

Stonefish sit at ocean bottoms. They look like stones. Their spines lie flat. They trick prey. Prey come close. Stonefish feel pressure. They attack. They open their spines. Their skin pulls away. They sting. Their spines cut victims. Sometimes humans step on them.

Stonefish kill most of their prey by catching them quickly after they've been stung.

Stonefish can sting out of water. They can live on the beach. They can be out of water for 24 hours.

Chapter seven

BLUE-RINGED OCTOPUSES

Blue-ringed octopuses live in the Pacific Ocean. They live in the Indian Ocean. They're dangerous ocean animals. They have small bites. Victims might not know they've been bit. But their poison is dangerous.

Their poison could kill 26 people. It takes minutes. Their poison is stronger than a powerful poison called cyanide. It's 10,000 times stronger than cyanide. Victims can't move. They can't see. Their brains stop working.

Blue-ringed octopuses are the only octopuses that are poisonous to humans.

The octopus's poison is part of its spit. Two glands make it. The glands are as big as its brain. Germs live in its glands. These germs live in groups. They make the poison.

Blue-ringed octopuses hide in rocks, sands, coral, and seaweed.

Blue-ringed octopuses mainly hunt crabs. They can hunt prey far away. They spit out poison. The poison makes a cloud. They trap prey in clouds. They wait. The prey dies.

They can hunt prey close to them. They jump. They grab prey. They use their arms. They pull prey toward their mouths. They have a horny beak. They bite down. They release poison. They stun prey's muscles. Prey can't breathe. Prey can't move.

These octopuses are about 8 inches (20.3 cm) long. They have yellow skin. They have brown spots. They blend in. But they change when in danger. They develop bright blue and black rings.

WHEN ANIMALS ATTACK!

Bees, wasps, and hornets are little. But they kill 60 people a year. They kill more people than sharks, crocodiles, and snakes combined. Some people die from shock. They're allergic to stings. Only female wasps sting. Wasps can sting several times. Their stingers don't fall off after use. Wasps' stings usually wear off in a day. But some people react very badly. Wasp venom can kill some people. Lucie Roussel was a mayor in Canada. She walked over a wasps' nest. She was stung 15 times. They stung her legs. She was rushed to the hospital. She died. Mark Evison also died from wasp stings. He lived in England. He was a farmer. He was working on a trench. He was digging. He disturbed a wasps' nest. Wasps attacked him. He crawled home. He called his brother. He said, "The wasps have got me!" He asked for help. It was too late. He died.

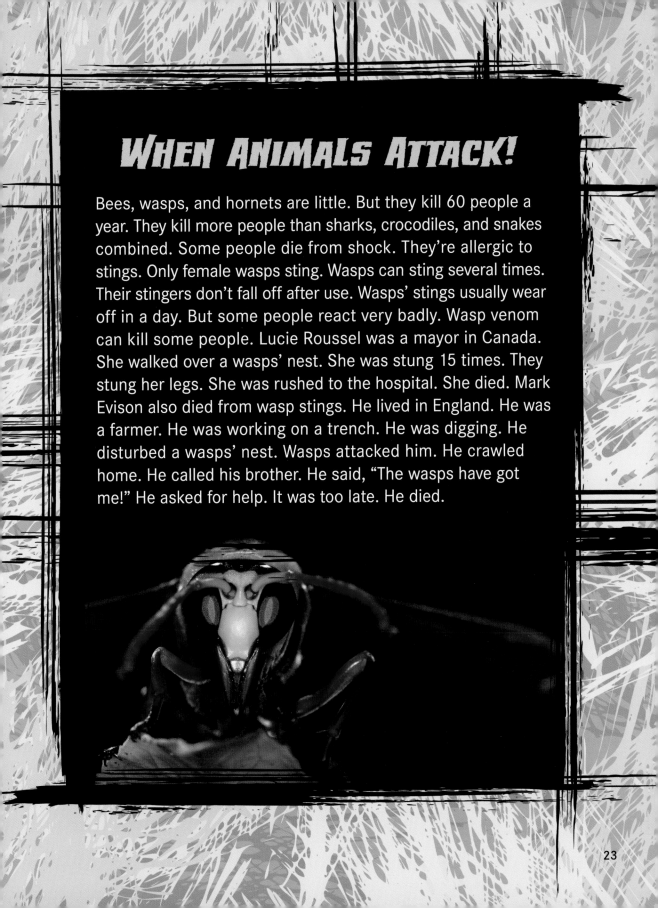

Chapter eight
CONE SNAILS

Cone snails are small. They eat meat. They're slow. They can't chase prey. They can't catch prey. But they have to eat. So they use poison. Their poison works quickly. Their poison is strong.

They're dangerous. They've killed more than 30 humans. Their poison affects body parts. It affects messages sent to brains.

They have a special tooth. It's like a needle. It's full of poison. They shoot their teeth at fish. They inject deadly poison. They kill prey. Their attacks take less than a second.

Cone snails grow to about 6 inches (15.2 cm).

Then they eat prey whole. They throw up scales. They
throw up bones.

Chapter nine

SEA SNAKES

Sea snakes live in the Pacific islands. They're related to cobras. They have short fangs. They have poison. Their poison is powerful. One drop can kill three men. Their poison is stronger than rattlesnake poison. It's stronger than king cobra poison.

Sea snakes can kill a man. They can do it in 6 to 12 hours. They don't have many predators. They're scary. Their poison acts fast. Victims can't swim away.

They're over 4 feet (1.2 meters) long. They have black and white stripes. Stripes trick the eyes. It looks like they're

Sea snakes have flat heads.
This helps them swim better.

moving the other way. Predators can't tell heads from tails. This gives sea snakes time. Sea snakes can run. Or they can fight.

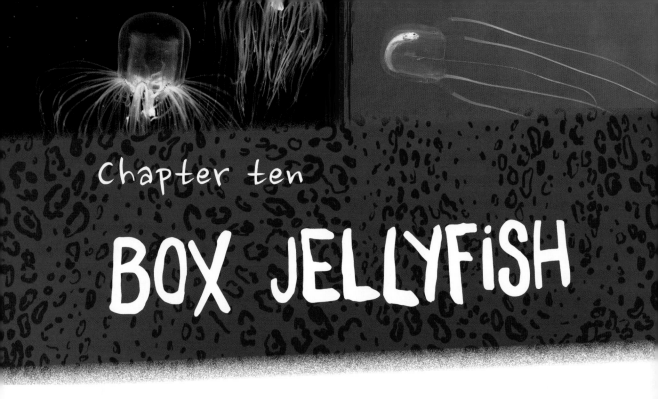

Chapter ten

BOX JELLYFISH

Deadly box jellyfish live in Australia. They're also called sea wasps. They're the world's most poisonous animals. One box jellyfish can kill 60 people. It can do this in minutes.

They have deadly **tentacles**. They have about 60. Tentacles are flexible arms. They can be 10 feet long (3 m). They have stinging cells. They have millions of stingers. The stingers are like tiny darts. They have poison.

Box jellyfish poison attacks hearts. It attacks spines. It attacks brains. It attacks skin cells. Victims can't move. Victims can die.

Victims have scars from box jellyfish. People say it's like being branded with red-hot irons.

Some humans have died. They didn't reach the shore. They didn't have time. Some survived. They still felt pain for weeks. They have many scars.

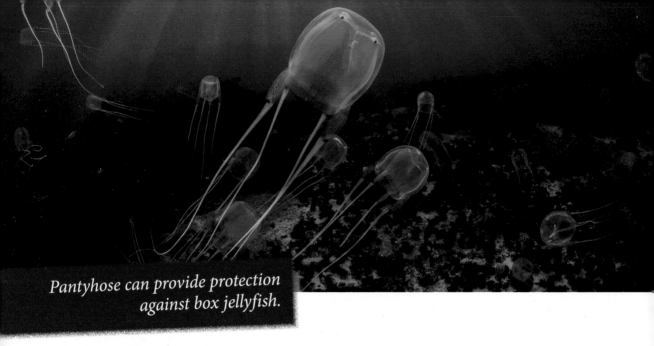

Pantyhose can provide protection against box jellyfish.

Box jellyfish are pale blue. They're clear. They're shaped like boxes. Victims don't feel stings. Victims do feel the poison.

They do great harm. They do this with a little touch. Their stingers cut through skin. They're like tiny knives. They inject poison. They stun. Victims can't move. They can't fight back. This protects their tentacles. Otherwise victims could snap off tentacles. Box jellyfish don't want this to happen.

Box jellyfish are smarter than other jellyfish. They have four brains. They see well. They have groups of eyes. Their eyes are on each side of their body.

DID YOU KNOW...?

- Some people get bee venom therapy. They want to get stung. They think bee stings heal.

- Some zookeepers clip stingers from stingrays. This doesn't hurt the stingrays.

- Scientists use Gila monster spit. They put the venom in drugs. The drugs help people remember. They help with memory loss.

- Kanchana Ketkeaw is from Thailand. She set a world record. She spent 32 days inside a glass cage. She was with 3,400 scorpions. She was stung nine times. But she wasn't affected. She got used to venom. She spent seven years performing with animals with venom.

- Some restaurants serve poisonous fish. They serve puffer fish. If it's cooked wrong, people can die.

- Cone snail venom is used as a painkiller. Scientists think it's a thousand times more effective than morphine.

- One way of treating jellyfish stings is to use vinegar. Pour vinegar on the affected spots.

CONSIDER THIS!

TAKE A POSITION! Should we, as humans, be afraid of these venomous animals? Argue your point with reasons and evidence.

SAY WHAT? Explain how and why at least three animals use their venom.

THINK ABOUT IT! Animals seem to have different ways to protect themselves. Using venom is one of them. How do humans protect themselves?

LEARN MORE!
- Riehecky, Janet. *Poisons and Venom: Animal Weapons and Defenses*. Mankato, MN: Capstone Press, 2012.
- Singer, Marilyn. *Venom*. Minneapolis: Millbrook Press, 2014.

GLOSSARY

allergic (uh-LUR-jik) having a highly sensitive reaction to something

bills (BILZ) flat beaks

glands (GLANDZ) organs that ooze stuff

lancet (LAN-sit) a point that can prick or cut

mammals (MAM-uhlz) type of animals that have fur or hair, give birth to live young, feed milk to babies, and are warm-blooded

pincers (PIN-surz) claws

predators (PRED-uh-turz) hunters

prey (PRAY) animals hunted for food

sac (SAK) bag or pouch

spurs (SPURZ) platypus stingers at their heels

survive (sur-VIVE) to stay alive

tentacles (TEN-tuh-kuhlz) flexible arms

venom (VEN-uhm) poison injected under the skin

victims (VIK-tuhmz) targets of attacks

INDEX

The animal kingdom is filled with some pretty wild creatures. Each book in the Wild Wicked Wonderful series counts down the top ten animals in categories like Stinkers and Venom. From great white sharks to naked mole rats, this series gives you an up close look at some of the world's most extreme animals. They're WILD. They're WICKED. And they're totally WONDERFUL.

BOOKS IN THIS SERIES

Top 10: Biters

Top 10: Daredevils

Top 10: Disguises

Top 10: Eaters

Top 10: Oddities

Top 10: Predators

Top 10: Stinkers

Top 10: Venom

45TH PARALLEL PRESS TITLES FEATURE:

High interest topics with accessible reading levels

Considerate vocabulary

Engaging content and fascinating facts

Clear text and formatting

Compelling photos

ISBN-13: 978-1-63470-627-8
90000
9 781634 706278

45th
Parallel
Press